The POLITICALLY INCORRECT Joke Book!

D1414097

by Four White Males

THE POLITICALLY INCORRECT JOKE BOOK

Twisted Humor with a Political Bent

by Four White Males being:
Charles "Al" Human, Jr., Joey West,
Greg Aunapu, and Biff Wellington
with Michael Matteo

Illustrations by Todd Schowalter

To all genuine cynics,
to whom nothing
is ever truly revealed.

Acknowledgements

Thanks are due to Joe Ajlouny, Dave Hornstein, Lisa A. McDonald, Charles A. Human, Sr., Lillian Human, Buddy E. Reese, Jr. and the Reese family, and especially to Marilyn Krol of Highway Graphics, Inc. Extra special thanks to Joseph and Ned for their superb politically incorrect judgment in sponsoring this project.

The dedication is a bastardization of an Oscar Wilde quote, to whose memory this book is affectionately and appropriately dedicated.

Copyright 1992 JSA Publications, Inc.
All rights reserved.
No part of this book may be used or reprinted without the advance written permission of the publisher.

Published by Push/Pull/Press,
an imprint of JSA Publications, Inc.
P.O. Box 37175 Oak Park, MI 48237

Printed in the United States of America
2 3 4 5 6 7 8 9 0

Cover Art by Todd Schowalter
Cover Design by Biff Wellington

ISBN: 0-929957-07-5
Library of Congress Catalog Number: 92-80466

Additional copies of this and other Push/Pull/Press
humor books are available by calling toll free
1-800-345-0096

Contents

Statement of Equal Treatment

How to Offend...

For You!

The Politically Incorrect Joke Book is an equal opportunity destroyer and does not discriminate on the basis of race, color, religion, national origin, age, gender, sexual preference, or handicap in its satirical practices. Furthermore, *The Politically Incorrect Joke Book* is an Affirmative Action joke book and actively recruits a demographically-representative pool of Politically Correct prudes, thin-skins, busy-bodies, and prigs as the butts of its humor.

Foreword

In The Beginning when God created the universe He had no idea that He was being politically incorrect. How could He make a man first? How could He put resources on the planet which would one day be used to pollute the earth? How could He exist, knowing that one day atheists would complain about His name being on U.S. currency? How could He create conservative Republicans?

What, you ask, is Political Correctness? Political Correctness is a social phenomenon that is the herpes virus of American culture. It is based upon the ideology that everything bad in society is the fault of Eurocentrism and that the acceptability of art, literature, television, history, etc. should be determined by societal misfits who have made a career out of mindless protests which score −5 on the "important things to worry about list."

The Goals of Political Correctness:

---

1. The elimination of all judgmental terms that are used by people to degrade, stigmatize, and offend members of different races, sexes, ethnic groups, religions, political organizations, or socially alternative lifestyles. (noted exception: White Heterosexual Males)
2. The development of a culturally sensitive review board to judge the acceptability of questionable jokes, gestures, music videos, television programs, thoughts, and words that may be construed as culturally inappropriate.
3. The creation of the *Speech Police,* a well trained squad of politically correct individuals who have taken classes in hypersensitivity training, censorship 101, Advanced Degrading of Western Civilization Historical Figures, and white heterosexual, male bashing.
4. Androgynous bathrooms based upon bathroom conduct. ("Sitting" and "Standing" Rooms will replace gender biased bathroom signs.)

A typical classified ad for PC recruits might look like this:

WANTED: Creative problem makers. If you like to whine, make a big deal about nothing, and want to get national attention this is the career for you. Qualifications: being easily offended, the ability to blame society for all social problems, and a strong desire to impose your social agenda on the American public. To apply call 1-800-WE-BITCH and listen for our recorded message:

"Welcome to the world of political correctness. Politically select behavior is the ideology that the acceptable usage of specific words and phrases are solely based upon the speakers' group affiliations. Please commit the following definition of Tolerance to memory—Tolerance is allowing other people to speak, act, and think in a manner that you approve of. Anything outside of these boundaries is unacceptable and politically unsuitable."

PC professionals take great care in selecting their complaint targets. First and foremost, PC'ers have focused on a complete overhaul of vocabulary. This is known as selective "vocabulary identification" or "word norming." It is the reason why perverts are being renamed morally repressed people and why males do not dare utter the words withdrawal, insertion, or penetration within 50 yards of women. Nothing is safe when a PCer is nearby. Sexual harassment will be any conduct that can be construed as mentally or physically suggestive on the part of males against females. Stares that span more than three seconds are prima facie evidence of sexual harassment.

So why have we endeavored to put this book together risking the wrath of the PC Horde? Because, being four white males, we are, by definition, politically incorrect. We like: doing the Tomahawk chop, throwing styrofoam in the ocean, calling women "broads," celebrating Columbus Day, criticizing the welfare system, voting for Republicans, benefiting from capitalism, praying in school, taunting zoo animals, making bumper stickers out of rain forest trees, and using the words Indian and Negro. But most of all we enjoy tormenting paranoid, self involved, anal retentive whiners with persecution complexes. Enjoy.

Michael A. Matteo
Tampa, Fla.

Introduction
Are You
Politically
Incorrect?

If you have this book in your hands now, we can accurately infer either one of two things: one, you value books enough to give us your time and money, or two, you have enough surplus capital and compassion to spend on things you don't particularly like. Either way, in an age where people get their information from eight-second sound bites, in an age where House Bank and S & L drafts are nothing but bungee parchment, the fact you have purchased this book makes you a special person whose way of life deserves protection.

Protection? From what you may ask. From a trendy brood which seeks to destroy your way of life, that's who! We call them the Political Correctness Horde.

To get an idea of what the Political Correctness Horde really is, first take a look at your checkbook. Now, imagine a horde that seeks to take and destroy, not just this book or your checkbook, but everything in the past 5,000 years which made them possible. That means everything from the written word, to printing by movable type, to the Industrial and Scientific Revolutions which created books and the leisure time to read them, to language standards, to individual rights of life, liberty, property, even on up to the most fundamental notions of free will and objective reality. Imagine even further that the Horde seeks to destroy these things on the pretext of every manner of racial, ethnic, sexual, linguistic and ideological whimsy conceivable.

If you can imagine this, then imagine no more. Our 5,000 year-old body of thought, effort, and finished result *is* Western Civilization. The Horde seeking to destroy it is a very real hodge-podge collection of Marxists, radical feminists, Jim Crow reverse-racists, Custers in feathers, limpwrists with bullwhips, and deconstructionist Nazis with power and influence over college campuses across the land and hungry for more.

And just when you think this group couldn't be sillier with their long list of complaints, you can't help but notice that the Politically Correct among us aren't even very representative of Non-Western peoples. While Russians and East Europeans try to emulate Western political and economic freedoms, the Marxist-like PC gang insist on damning the West as an "oppressive" culture. While Black South Africans giddily wait for Western-style products and franchises, but mostly Western-style liberties, the Afro-centrist PCers would have us believe that Western culture and discrimination stick together, pardon the pun, like white on rice. And while women under Islam aspire for driving licenses within their cloak-cloistered heads, the PC Femi-Nazis castigate going out into society to see and be seen.

We could go on. We have not mentioned animal rights groups, nor gay activists, nor police bashers, and so on *ad nauseum*. We think our point has been made. That's why you deserve protection! For Political Correctness is like a rabid cult religion, complete with its own sacred myths, clergy, totems, ju-jus, sacraments, and for the infidel who doesn't believe ardently enough, its own thought-controlling lynch mob.

Since keelhauling is not a legal option for dealing with the Politically Correct, we have done the next best thing: opened the door of ridicule to them. That is the purpose of this loose collection of Politically Incorrect humor. We trust you'll conclude we have succeeded.

As an added service, we have prepared the following multiple choice test to help you determine if you're one of us. We trust you are. If by chance you are not, drop dead!

There is considerable confusion over what it means to be Politically Incorrect. The object is to be as incorrect as possible, but in this world of uncertainty, how can you be sure you've got it wrong? After consulting with a panel of experts (consisting of ourselves) we have devised the following test. So you know there are no tricks, the test is a series of questions and answers on common everyday events. Just select the response that best fits your prejudices. Add up your points after you are done to determine your Political Incorrectness Approval Rating.

1. During a casual conversation, a friend makes a racist remark. You should:
   a. Punch his lights out.
   b. Nonchalantly change the subject.
   c. Give him the phone number of the local KKK chapter.

2. A popular Republican president is to speak at your university commencement ceremonies. You should:
   a. Carry a picket sign and boo loudly throughout the address.
   b. Sleep, but be careful not to snore through his speech.
   c. Cheer at his every remark with unbridled enthusiasm.

3. While walking leisurely through your neighborhood you see Operation Rescue attempting to blockade the local Planned Parenthood clinic. You should:
   a. Push the demonstrators aside so medical personnel and pregnant women can enter.
   b. Turn around and discreetly walk away.
   c. Offer your car as part of their barricade.

4. You notice a heroic bronze statue of General George Custer in your town square. You should:
   a. Melt the thing down at night and donate the scrap proceeds to the nearest tribal school.
   b. Count the number of pigeon droppings on it and move along.
   c. Polish it to a brilliant finish and lay a wreath in memory of his regiment.

5. While driving down the street you see a man standing on the corner holding a sign reading: "Will Work 4 Food." You should:
   a. Offer him a ride, hand him $10 for dinner and let him keep the change.

    b. Just pass by and avoid eye contact.

    c. Jump the curb and attempt to run the bum over.

6. During a visit to the zoo you see a lion pacing forlornly in his cage. You should:

    a. Open the cage and set him free.

    b. Turn away and go buy a hot dog.

    c. Tease and taunt the lion unmercifully for not appreciating his taxpayer-paid meals.

7. During a hike in the woods you notice a smoldering abandoned campfire. You should:

    a. Put the fire out.

    b. Run like hell and call Smokey the Bear.

    c. Fan it into a forest fire to get those lazy park rangers off their butts.

8. A Haitian refugee appears unexpectedly at your door begging for political asylum. You should:

    a. Take him in and hide him away from the authorities.

    b. Close the door and hope he goes away.

    c. Immediately turn him into the Immigration and Naturalization Service and file a complaint against your local police for not arresting him first.

9. A leading televangelist is caught in a sex scandal. You should:

    a. Rejoice that hypocrisy has been exposed.

    b. Yawn and take it with a grain of apathy.

    c. Contribute money to his legal defense fund.

10. While browsing through the bookstore you stumble across this book. You should:

    a. Demand the manager pull it off the shelves.

b. Ignore it as harmless.

c. Buy a hundred copies for all your conservative friends.

To establish your Political Incorrectness Approval Rating score 10 points for each time you answered C, five points for every B answer and zero points for each time you answered A.

If your score is 33 or lower then you're obviously a left-wing do gooder bore. You're so politically correct that you are clearly no fun to be around.

If your score is 34–66 then you obviously have no sense of political commitment. Why are you bothering to read this book anyway? You must be a loser or an apathetic creep.

If your score is 67 or higher, you passed the test. Congratulations! You're 100 percent Politically Incorrect and are clearly qualified for a job with any Republican administration or conservative think-tank.

1

The Politically Incorrect Joke Sampler

—What do you call a Politically Correct male American?
  Either a eunuch or a suicide.

—What do you call a Politically Correct American female?
  You just don't!

—What do you call a Politically Correct teacher?
  An oxymoron.

—Which third-person pronoun best describes a Politically Correct person?
  He/she/it.

—What kind of computer has no system of logic, rewrites what you've input and exhibits selective memory?
   A PC Compatible.

—What does S & M mean to PC people?
   Sartre and Marx.

—What does a politically incorrect male sobbingly confess to a PC sexual bondage queen?
   "Overthrow me baby, for the Oppressive Objectifying Male I am!"

—What is the Politically Correct idea of foreplay?
   Catching a sanitized hackey sack between the knees.

—Of all the rights that advocates of PC-think create, which is the most dangerous?
   Bragging rights.

—What did Edward Kennedy reply when asked if he would run for president again?
   "I'll drive off that bridge when I get to it."

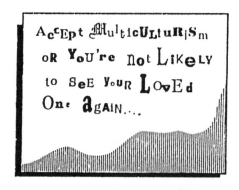

—What's putrid and smelly in public libraries?
   Homeless readers.

—What does a PC person call his or her spouse, girlfriend, boy-friend or lover?
   An insignificant other.

—Why didn't George Washington's father punish him for cutting down the cherry tree?
   Because young George was still holding the axe.

—What do sex and smoking a cigarette have in common?
   It's getting so you can't do either except in the bedroom.

—How is having a happy childhood like committing a crime?
   You could be arrested for either.

—What's the difference between Ape Man and PC Man?
   Ape Man swallows his victims after chewing them up.

—How does a Democrat define his political philosophy?
   "I disagree with Republicans!"

—How many feminists does it take to change a lightbulb?
   Two, one to change it and the other to tell her what a great job she did.

—How many Black activists does it take to register a voter?
   Three, one to register, the other to harass the city clerk, and the last to call the U.S. Civil Rights Commission.

—What do gratuitous sex and violence have in common?
   They can both be seen nightly on network television.

—What's the best argument for having mandatory dress codes in the public schools?

To prevent kids from shooting each other over their shoes and coats.

—Why are "attack ads" indispensible in American election campaigns?

Because the so-called "politically correct" make great targets.

—What's the newest dirty word in the dictionary?

Incumbent.

—What do you call ten PC persons in the express checkout at the grocery store?

An air line.

—Which four words are uttered for no apparent reason other than to inflame the passions of PC advocates?

Capital Gains Tax Cut.

—How is passing out condoms in school like the Congressional check-bouncing scandal?

You could call either "Rubbergate."

—How is the Soviet Union like the walls of Jericho?

Both miraculously came tumbling down.

—How can you tell a gun-control advocate from a mouse?

A mouse has more backbone.

—What does a PC person do upon being mugged by a Latino gang?

Apologizes for not wearing his gold watch, which they could have stolen too.

—What do green weeds, bean mash and soy fungus have in common?

They can each be found on the menu of your neighborhood macrobiotic cafe.

—What liberal special interest group most strongly supports the Save the Whales campaign?
Fat feminists.

2

Politically Incorrect Observations

Did you ever notice that . . .

—Women who complain about being treated as sex objects often look like refrigerators with heads?

—Multi-cultural classes always praise abolitionist Frederick Douglass, who incidentally looked upon the supposedly racist U.S. Constitution with considerable admiration?

—Feminist studies classes extol mythical goddesses as role models, yet learn about them from "chauvanist, sexist" Greco-Roman authors like Aristophanes, Homer and their ilk?

—Native American militants maintain that violence against their people started with the arrival of Europeans, despite the fact that human

Employers who engage in "Race-norming" really mean they've set up hiring quotas.

"Gender-blending" is another way of saying tokenism.

A "Conscientious Objector" is another name for a pacifist or a draft dodger.

When speaking or reading of "Native Americans," they mean Indians.

"Supporters of Reproductive Rights" are really just abortion/pro-choice advocates.

"Non-traditional Partner Participants" are gays and lesbians.

"Sufferers of Post-HIV Complications" are people with the AIDS virus.

Those among us who are described as "Successful Correctional Detainees" are actually ex-cons.

"Secular Humanists" are agnostics and atheists.

4

PC Speak

The onslaught of PC-think has had a somewhat debilitating influence on our vocabulary. We must now contend (and comprehend) PC-speak. The following is a brief glossary of neo-PC terminology for those of you who have not yet been indoctrinated. (To better acclimate yourself we have included some doozies from the past too.)

A "Victim of Involuntary Servitude" means a slave.

"Pregnancy Termination" is a fancy way of saying abortion.

You practice a "Non-discriminating Sexual Orientation" if you are a bi-
    sexual.

The "G" word:	Gay
The "H" word:	Homosexuality
The "I" word:	Intellectualism
The "J" word:	Japan (As in "Japan Bashing")
The "K" word:	Klan (As in "Ku Klux")
The "L" word:	Liberal
The "M" word:	Multi-culturalism
The "N" word:	Native (As in "Native American")
The "O" word:	Ozone
The "P" word:	Patriotism
The "Q" word:	Queer
The "R" word:	Racism
The "S" word:	Safe-sex (Formerly "Socialism")
The "T" word:	Tribalism
The "U" word:	Unitarianism (Formerly "Ultra-liberal")
The "V" word:	Vivisectionism
The "W" word:	Western (As in "Western Civilization")
The "X" word:	X-mas
The "Y" word:	Yuppie
The "Z" word:	Zoology

3

The PC Alphabet

As we are all too plainly aware, the English alphabet has been made a veritable minefield in the PC war. We all know what the "L" word stands for. Let's take a look at the other letters in our once noble alphabet.

The "A" word:	Affirmative Action (Formerly "Anti-nuke")
The "B" word:	Bio-degradable
The "C" word:	Condom (Formerly "Communism")
The "D" word:	De-constructionism
The "E" word:	Ethno-centrism
The "F" word:	Feminism

—Every time something goes wrong in a Republican administration the Congress is quick to call for the appointment of a Special Prosecutor?

HYPHENATED AMERICAN CULTURE CENTER

torture, sacrifice and cannibalism were common traditions among the natives of the "New World?"

—Afro-Americans who routinely say "It's a black thang, you woo'dn't understand," never understand themselves why they sadly remain stuck in that "black thang"—commonly called a ghetto?

—There's always something half-assed about hyphenated PC phrases?

—So-called hyphenated-Americans (as in "Italian-American") never think about calling people by their first names, like Tom, Dick or Harry?

—Readers and writers who use race and gender as an indicia of literary merit wouldn't know literature if it bit them in their fannies?

—Gays who complain about the lack of representation in Western culture have conveniently "discovered" Plato, Homer and Alexander the Great, among others, may have been homosexuals themselves?

—Calls to teach Black English Vernacular are typically made by civil rights activists who speak flawlessly. Thus we can comprehend but not understand them?

—To ardent feminists, a woman's "crowning glory" is the hair on her legs and arm pits?

—The one thing environmentalists recycle best is their repetitive doom-saying claptrap?

—In the saying: "If you're not a part of the solution, you're a part of the problem," the solution is always worse and more expensive than the problem itself?

—Sports teams with Native American nicknames, like the Washington Redskins, the Atlanta Braves, etc., only come under attack to change their names when they start winning?

—Women leftists are more annoying than male leftists?

People's Democratic Republics (what few are left) are communist totalitarian regimes.

A "Family Planning Center" is in reality a front office for numerous state paid abortion clinics.

A "Political Action Committee" is really a special interest lobby's slush fund.

Groups organized under names like "Citizens for Safer Streets" or "United Community Coalition for True Law and Order" are in reality police bashers.

Short people are better called "Vertically Challenged" so their feelings don't get hurt.

Likewise, the physically handicapped are "Physically Challenged" and the mentally retarded are either "Emotionally Challenged," "Psychologically Repressed" or people suffering from "Organic Concussion Syndrome."

Race riots (yes, they occasionally still occur) are now called "Failures of Community Cohesion" or "Breakdowns of Neighborly Accommodations."

You're undergoing psychiatric treatment if you're "Searching for Your Inner Child."

Rapists aren't criminals so much as they are men who engage in "Violent Phallo-centricity."

Cynics are more aptly called De-constructionists due to their heightened sensitivity to the norms of conventional wisdom.

Non-white residents of America are more appropriately known as "People of Color."

Those who champion first amendment rights would prefer not to be called flag burners or criminal rights advocates, but "Libertarians," "Freedom Patriots," and "Bill of Rightists."

"Congregate Care-Giving Shelters" are actually prison half-way houses.

A public school kid who doesn't understand English is a "Linguistic Minority."

5

Having Fun with the Politically Correct

If we wrote in the 'don't-step-on-any-toes' style prevalent today, we would say that the Political Correctness crowd is not exactly a group of people whose thoughts can change with rational discourse. But since our literary style steps on toes, kicks shins, knees groins, and pulls hair, we'll say that nursing home inmates who believe that Apollo 11 was fake and wrestling is real have a better grasp of reality than the Politically Correct: the old fogies at least have some notion of truth and falsehood, however warped.

So since the Politically Correct aren't going to change (but are sure out to change you for the worse), we say have fun with them.

Here for your vengeful jollies, are some of the ways you can keep different exponents of Political Correctness from getting you down.

When a Politically Correct clone accuses you of insensitivity towards women, minorities, religious groups, homosexuals, the handicapped, etc., act in a spirit of *true* tolerance and say: 'I don't hate (women, minorities, religious groups, homosexuals, the handicapped, etc.), I just hate *you!*

If an Afrocentrist tells you that black Africans created the first airplane, ask this person if black Africans also created the first ticket lines, the first airline food, the first airport Moonies, the first air traffic controller's unions, the first skyjackings, the first DC-10s, the first Luftwaffe . . .

When a radical feminist inevitably tells you that: 'You just don't get it!', respond like this: 'Well, judging from your looks, I'd say that *you* don't get it either!'

If you have the misfortune of taking an English course with a deconstructionist professor, argue in your first paper that deconstructionist course loads are forms of linguistic oppression and should be abolished. While deconstructionists are not known for consistency, you can't go wrong, regardless of the outcome. If the professor is inconsistent, your paper will get his goat; if the professor is consistent, the professor will take your advice and everyone in class will have credit for a crypt course in doodling and/or studying for other classes.

Tell a radical feminist that she has been made a contestant in a velcro wall-climbing contest . . . and that, for her, no suit is necessary.

You can torment your deconstructionist English professor even further by turning your desk away from the professor. When the professor tells the class about the exam and says: 'You're going to have to study for this and I mean it!', turn around and say: 'You mean it?' Surprise! Surprise! You just destroyed your entire curriculum!'

Next time an Afrocentrist propagates the questionable notion that a single African woman gave birth to mankind, take some inspiration from the movie *Arthur* and tell him: 'Well, she'd have to have been a very big woman!'

Wear a T-shirt saying proudly that: 'I'm Part of the Problem.'

If, by now that same old deconstructionist professor is still badgering you with his curriculum, you still have a chance to have some real fun with the idiot. If he's a European in his 70s or 80s, just ask him about 'the war.' His pants are guaranteed to turn several shades darker and his face will change a whiter shade than even he would desire. With any luck, at this point, an undercover officer of the Mossad posing as a student will dismiss class forever.

6

PC and Original Sin

Original Sin was once an anathema to our Judeo-Christian culture, particularly those of us who professed to be practicing Catholics. Yet in a PC world, the concept has virtually disappeared. What follows are examples of PC justifications for such sins.

Abortion can be permitted because it is not murder. An unborn is not a human life in the "Biblical sense."

Homosexuality is not sodomy or anything of the sort. Today's society is far too advanced to be bound by the prudish views of some unknown Biblical contributor.

Materialism and selfishness are to be encouraged. It's good for the economy.

Telling lies is justifiable to keep secrets like the existence of extramarital affairs, criminal embezzlement, illegal governmental wire-tapping, and scores of other nasty, but lamentably tolerated activities. After all, it's been said a million times, "What we don't know won't hurt us!"

Theft, frequently termed larceny and understood by most to be wrong, is excused when the perpetrator is a homeless vagabond or recently laid-off auto worker.

Adultery is frequently justified by the participants as a kind of "safety valve" with the purpose of protecting the family unit from disruption. Why divorce the wife if you can get what you want by fooling around with the barmaid? Surely the kids will turn out better if they don't come from a broken home.

Fornication, long regarded by all major faiths as sinful, is now rather fashionable. And, it is made pure by the need to control sexual activity due to the spread of AIDS. It's okay to screw around if you don't do it very much and always use a condom.

Suicide is now the rage, especially if it's doctor-assisted. Never mind that it is sinful for the person and unethical for the doctor. It's justified by the high cost of medical treatment, the need for organ donors and the fact that most patients would have died long ago without the intervention of modern medicine.

An unchaste priesthood is now being advocated in the Catholic Church. It seems the sacrifice of a cleric's carnal instincts is not one of the kinds of devotions the apostles meant to include in establishing the precepts of a priestly vocation.

7

PC and Historical Revisionism

The revision of history is something better left to totalitarian dictatorships whose power rests upon undermining the contributions of others while glorifying their own. But PC-devotees have adopted the practice as their own. These examples of their efforts sufficiently illustrate this dangerous and nonsensical tendency.

Christopher Columbus was not the enchanted discoverer of the New World, he was its chief destroyer. For not only did he wrongly claim territory in the name of Spain, he also enslaved the native inhabitants, robbed them of their bounty and ignited an era of war and strife unequaled prior to the 20th century.

European missionaries that followed the explorers to the Americas didn't respect the beliefs and customs of the native peoples. Never mind that those customs included cannibalism, among other things.

Americans settled the West not as pioneers but as trespassing militants. They continually stole land from Native Americans, and broke treaties for territories they previously agreed to respect.

Vladimir Lenin and Mao Tse-tung were not criminal tyrants but revolutionary philosophers dedicated to ending hunger and exploitation.

World War I, the so-called war to end all wars, was caused by immoral and jealous imperialists fighting over their conflicting colonial interests.

The hunger and poverty throughout Africa is not a result of geographical or climatic conditions but of the gerrymandered frontiers drawn by distrusting colonial governors in the 19th century and Cold War theatrics in the 20th.

The Biblical account of history is patently false and inherently illogical. Besides, Darwin's evolutionism is far more intellectually stimulating than God and creationism.

The atomic bombing of Hiroshima and Nagasaki in World War II was not an effort to shorten the war or save American lives. It was instead an attempt to experiment with nuclear energy and radioactive fallout on "real life" targets.

John F. Kennedy was a great liberal who would have never allowed the U.S. to get involved in Vietnam.

Historically the Bishops of Rome, better known as the Popes, have been corrupt and lecherous old men with more interest in their indiscretions with young boys than advancing the faith.

Communism provided a basis for Third World nations to organize and break away from their imperial/colonial experiences.

One-party rule, of whatever political persuasion, is a necessary step on the path to democracy.

8

All God's Creatures

We all remember the infamous Snail Darter case. It arose in 1972 as a consequence of the planned construction and operation of a hydro-electric dam in Tennessee. Proponents of the dam argued that the project would provide much needed electricity to the area; opponents claimed no amount of electricity could justify the permanent destruction of the Snail Darter's habitat. The case eventually made its way to the U.S. Supreme Court, which held in favor of the Snail Darter, saying Congress did not make any exceptions to the enforcement provisions of the Endangered Species Act. It proved to be a precedent for more than the lowly fishling. Since 1976, a slew of similar cases have circled their way through both federal and state courts and administrative agencies, leading often to ridiculous results.

—Conservationists in the State of Washington have waged a decade long battle to preserve forests for the benefit of the Spotted Owl. Though many compromise plans have been discussed which protect certain tracts, mandate the study of the impact of lumber harvesting on the eco-system of the forests, and set aside a portion of the proceeds for wildlife trust funds, little progress has been made in resolving the dispute. Despite the lumber industries' assertion that the prohibition against felling trees will cost as many as ten thousand jobs, the conservationists have thus far prevailed. The Canadian government, having a far less resistant and organized conservation movement, has chosen to take advantage of the situation by increasing its raw lumber subsidy, thus boosting exports at the expense of American workers.

—Nuclear energy enthusiasts, ever anxious to end our dependence on foreign oil, have long advocated the development of additional nuclear plants around the country. Anti-nuke forces, comprising of

ALL GOD'S CREATURES....

hodge-podge coalitions of conservationists, environmentalists, ecologists, hunters, leftists, concerned homeowners, and others, have scuttled all but a handful. They have done so by effectively appealing to mass emotions on a range of issues from safety to cost. Thankfully, they rarely forget God's little creatures in preparing their one-sided environmental impact studies. As a result, the U.S. remains heavily dependent on imported oil, the single greatest drain on our foreign exchange reserves. In addition, most public utilities continue to burn coal, which as we all know, causes air pollution, acid rain and strip mining. The animals don't seem to mind them as much.

—The University of Arizona recently escaped the total scrapping of its ambitious telescope project atop Mt. Graham. The cost? University officials agreed not to disturb the "delicate" nesting grounds of the Western Red Squirrel, a pesky little species that inhabits the mountain's early slopes. Though the exact cost of modifications in the project has yet to be determined, initial estimates are in the low millions. The added cost to the tuition for students could be as much as $200 per year, thanks to a challenge by the Sierra Club Legal Defense Fund. Until the squirrels abandon their habitat, that is.

More recently, the Mt. Graham project has been derailed once again, this time by a splinter Apache group calling itself the Apache Survival Coalition. The A.S.C. claims Emerald Peak, the specific site of the three telescope project, is part of a sacred burial ground. It's important to note that the majority of the Apache Nation in Arizona disagrees with this assertion. Naturally, any resolution of the controversy will only take place after millions are wasted in litigation, money the Apache could doubtlessly find better uses for.

—Alaska has proven petroleum reserves to sustain American de-
mand for over one hundred years. Despite this, anti-development
organizations have fought tooth and nail against the expansion of oil
drilling in Alaska's frozen steppes. Though no one can doubt their
sincerity, many doubt their wisdom. The 1989 Exxon-Valdez oil spill
proved nature's incredible resiliency when faced with disaster. Yet,
conservationists insist the "fragile" environment is at risk, that Alaska's birds, bears and other wildlife are threatened with extinction.
Meanwhile, America and much of the rest of the world stand almost
entirely incapable of influencing the volatile cost and supply of oil.

—California, Louisiana and Texas have felt the impact on their
economies of the on-again, off-again rush to explore for petroleum
and natural gas by off-shore drilling. The cause? Environmentalists
who care more about the quality of life for fish than the nation's
economy and security. Oil spills and resultant water pollution, they
say, will do more damage than we can afford to risk. When pressed
for examples to illustrate their points, environmentalists and their
supporters cite study after study to support their contentions. Oil
companies rebut each study with studies of their own. The dispute
rages, even as all three states face mounting budget deficits and
unemployment. Meanwhile, in much of the Third World, automobile
owners wait in line for days to get their meager gasoline rations.

—State park officials in Florida have been stumped over their attempts to preserve vast portions of the Everglades regions for the
benefit of hundreds of species of animals. Wildlife groups have
charged the state with recklessly disregarding hundreds of other
species of fish, fowl, reptiles, and yes, even insects. It seems the
groups are convinced the state preserves are only being offered as a

first step in long term plans to sell thousands of acres to recreational and hospitality development types. Though state officials categorically deny any such motive, the controversy ensues. Meanwhile, all the animal species the state sought to protect from encroachment remain prey to hunters and thrill seekers. It makes one wonder who's on which side of the issues?

9

Politically Incorrect
Motion Pictures

We've all seen lots of movies that make no attempt to hide their politically correct sentiments. This got us to thinking. Why not propose some variations on the themes espoused therein? Though they might be panned by unscrupulous film critics in the pay of liberal Hollywood-types, we're confident enough people across the nation would pay to see them. Please also purchase the videos too, our allies need all the help they can get.

Boyz 'N The Hoods

Lousiana's David Duke stars as the charismatic young leader of a community help organization—the KKK. When he later develops

political ambitions, he discovers that his wild-eyed idealism is misunderstood. He is thus forced to run against his own spotted past. Will he rock the Washington establishment or crumble his own power-base? David Dinkins cameos in the role of the president of the NAACP. A powerful drama. ★★★

Do the Right Wing

An action-packed political thriller about a brash and courageous presidential hopeful whose economic policies feature a new and powerful tool to balance the budget deficit. Called "Quantum Mathematics," this number crunching technological innovation has the secret capability of falsely projecting the loser as the winner. His scheme is ultimately exposed by a Young Republicans group on the eve of election day. Starring John Sununu as a hard-boiled Republican operative with an I.Q. no Democratic computer programmer can lick. Suspenseful, chilling. ★★★★

Screwing Miss Daisy

Rev. Al Sharpton plays a chauffeur who tries to prove his employer's rape claim in the face of evidence suggesting it is the product of her senile sexual fantasies. The alleged rapist, a freshman Republican Congressman from Iowa (played by Fred Grandy), struggles to make sense of the charges. After a cathartic trial, during which the defendant is exonerated with his reputation intact, Sharpton starts a crusade against the criminal justice system, claiming the phantom men of Miss Daisy's wet dream would have gone to prison if they were Black. Pat Buchanan stars as defense attorney Henry "Ace" Culpepper. ★★★

Terminator III

Shirley MacLaine reincarnates as a murderous robot from the future programmed to kill her previous incarnation before she can write several strange but bestselling books. Jerry Brown stars as the sta- lked star's protector, the mysterious Uzi-toting "Como." Though the storyline appears trite at first glance, the sheer delight of watching MacLaine attack herself is worth the price of a ticket alone. ★★

Die Hardest

Bruce Willis stars as a popular actor in an annoying and formulaic television cop show. The action turns when he stumbles into the role of an unlikely hero in a hit movie. In the midst of a skyrocketing career, he is felled by Sylvester Stallone Disease, a noxious fame-numbing ailment forcing him to make several terrible comedies. With his career shot and his mortgage in arrears, the actor resorts to hosting parades and telethons. He grudgingly accepts a position as host of a new game show, Name That Animal Bite. Though the audience sees his professional demise long before he does, Willis' manly breathing and hairy chest will make every woman lust for him, and every man feel a vicarious thrill machismo. ★★

The Big Spill

A group of oil company executives led by Arnold Schwarznegger take a hard look at their lives, à la "12 Angry Men," and conclude they really don't give a damn. Meanwhile, a coalition of environmentalists and conservationists (Ed Asner plays their nauseating leader) threaten to launch a campaign to seek indictments. Despite the script's cliche moments, this serio-comic offering causes us to question the capitalist in us all. ★★★

Spittoon

Oliver Stone's latest blockbuster in which popular baseball players rape their dates, beat their spouses and spit tobacco globs wherever they choose. Against this backdrop, salaries continue to raise to astronomical levels, and the players threaten to boycott the All-Star Game unless new stadium construction is completely publicly-financed. Though we are charmed by their boy-like antics, we are ultimately left asking them: "Say it ain't so." Lloyd Bensten co-stars in the role of a weak but supportive baseball commissioner. ★★★

Jingle Fever

Michael Jackson and Madonna play talented recording stars of different races but with a remarkable similarity in their sense of public outrage. The pair are drawn together by their inane fascination with their crotches, and by their desire to sell-out to multi-million dollar commercial sponsorships. They fall madly in love during a worldwide tour to end jock-itch. Tensions between them rise, however, when Jackson's character completes his metamorphosis (via a sexchange operation) into Diana Ross, played by herself. When he wins the Grammy for best female vocalist, an enraged Madonna pulls out a gun and. . . . Tragic but entertaining. ★★★★

10

PC Kennedy Assassination Conspiracy Theories

PC-chic was taken into another dimension with the release of Oliver Stone's film about the assassination of President Kennedy. It suddenly became fashionable to ridicule the Warren Commission's findings and discourse on this or that conspiracy theory. In case you were out of the country or in a coma at the time, the following is a list of the most commonly believed theories.

The Mafia killed JFK because the Justice Department was indicting many of their members. Others think the Mafia was behind the killing because the president refused to depose Fidel Castro, who had expropriated millions in Mafia-owned real estate, totally gutting their gambling and drug activities in Cuba. Anti-Castro Cubans based in Miami are thought to be involved in the plot. Still others think the conspiracy was hatched by the Mafia and Teamsters acting in concert. Jimmy Hoffa was said to be infuriated at his indictment (and subsequent conviction) by the Kennedy Administration for pension fund fraud. The mob was naturally pretty ticked too, since their operations came under scrutiny as a result of the charges.

The CIA was behind the assassination because Kennedy refused to match the Soviets missile to missile in the arms race. The FBI has also been fingered because Robert Kennedy, his older brother's Attorney General, was planning to retire J. Edgar Hoover. Others believe JFK was murdered by the FBI to prevent him from being blackmailed by any one of the vixens he was carrying on with.

Others believe the "government within the government" was responsible. Though nobody is sure who or what this secret cell of illegitimate rulers really is, they were likely motivated because Kennedy was reportedly planning to withdraw U.S. military advisers from South Vietnam. Suspected conspirators may have included members of the Secret Service, the Defense Intelligence Agency, the Joint Chiefs of Staff and the National Security Agency.

Some believe Castro wanted JFK dead because of Kennedy's own attempts on his life. We know there were several. Many think the Soviets are the logical culprits because of the humiliation they suffered over the Cuban Missile Crisis the year before. The KGB, we are told, has a thing against getting caught transporting nuclear warheads in the Caribbean Sea.

Though more lowly ranked, conspiratorialists have also indicted Vice President Lyndon B. Johnson, French heroin dealers, the Dallas Police, Puerto Rican nationalists and others for JFK's murder.

11

Animal Rights and Wrongs

Now that accepted standards of Human Rights have taken hold on much of the world, PC-champions have invented an illogical extension of the doctrine: animal rights. In the past several years, animal rightists of all stripes have come out of the proverbial woodwork to spread their new creed. They cite variations of the following in their crusade.

That recreational hunters and outdoorsmen are the modern day equivalents of beaver trappers. They kill animals for fun, for profit or to simply boost their masculine egos.

Zoos are the equivalent of prisons except the animals are not convicted felons. Sea World animals may be better fed, but that's only because they do as many as 15 shows per day. Circus trainers exploit and mistreat their animals in the name of show business.

Cattle and hog farmers treat their animals like stock-in-trade instead of as living things, their barns and transport vehicles are allegedly overcrowded and badly designed. Slaughterhouses use cruel and inhumane methods to kill animals for food processing. Animals are neglected, discriminated against and subject to annihilation at a whim.

Research laboratories in academia and industry routinely maim and torture animals in their experiments. Moreover, laboratory animals are implanted and infected with deadly substances, are kept in tiny cages and receive little if any consideration.

And yes even you, the pet owner, have fallen under the scrutiny of animal rights proponents. You may be criticized for failing to get your pets their shots. You may suffer insults if you neglect to groom or exercise them. Your pet license may even be revoked if your little poodle doesn't receive the level of love a reasonable person under like circumstance would offer.

SAVE A GERBIL TODAY!

12

PC and Reaganomics

PCers of all shades have much in common, but perhaps have no greater affinity than their shared contempt of the Reagan-Bush Administrations. The 1980's, we are reminded, were years of extravagance and profligration. Our economic growth, a spectacular bouquet of statistics, was deceptive and artificial in reality. Rather than being better off, they say, most of us are worse off now than we were under Jimmy Carter. Let's take a look at their most common complaints:

—The federal budget deficit is skyrocketing out of control even as social welfare programs have been eliminated or cut to the bone.

—Taxes are actually higher now than they've ever been, and the middle class is paying a greater percentage of their income in taxes than the wealthiest Americans.

—The U.S. does not need and cannot afford the multitude of weapons programs currently under contract by the Pentagon. Despite the end of the Cold War, the Reagan-Bush Administration continues to push for the "Star Wars" anti-missile system, the B-2 "Stealth" bomber, the MX "Peacekeeper" multi-warhead rocket and others.

—Since the Reagan-Bush Administration assumed power in The White House, Americans of all kinds have been pushed beneath the poverty line. Almost a million are said to be homeless, and millions of others have become "hidden homeless" because they've had to reside with their families because they can't afford a dwelling of their own.

—The S & L Scandal, the costliest financial crisis in American history, is the fault of Reagan-style regulatory cuts, crooked and greedy banking executives and over-indulgent (meaning Republican) speculation on worthless real estate and junk bonds. (It may be instructive to note that four of the five senators who were implicated in abetting the scandal were Democrats. The lone Republican was exonerated.)

—That merger-mania served the interests of a few fat-cat investors while gutting some of the nation's largest corporations. As a consequence, competition was lessened and millions were thrown out of work without the expectation of ever finding a similar job again.

—Race relations have worsened due to the Reagan-Bush Administrations' lip service to the cause of civil rights.

—State and local governments have been forced to raise taxes and cut spending because the federal government has let the bottom drop out of programs like revenue sharing, block grants and the like.

—Personal and business bankruptcies have exploded in number and magnitude as unemployment worsens and the burdens of debt (from easy to get credit) can no longer be tolerated.

—Police brutality has increased, and the nation is becoming plagued with neo-Nazi hate groups as a result of a general rise of intolerance and distrust against minorities and the socially under-privileged.

—America has entered a new era of saber-rattling and jingoistic browbeating following the collapse of Communism in Eastern Europe.

13

The New PC Curriculum

College campuses are the new PC battlefields, especially regarding attacks on "The Canon," the traditional core curriculum taught at most colleges and universities. The Canon is said to be outmoded, sexist and exclusionary in content, so much so that they claim nobody really gives a hoot about what Aristotle, Shakespeare, Dickens or Melville wrote about anything other than confessions for their sins. Below are new courses which have been suggested or contemplated to placate PC-minded students:

COURSE NAME	DEPARTMENT
The Homeless Experience	Humanities 103

COURSE NAME	DEPARTMENT
20th Century Damage Wrought by Western Democracies	Political Science 101
Third World Poetry Survey	Literature 205
Nurturing Your Inner Child	Psychology 102
The African-American Experience in the Reagan Years	Black Studies 214
The Economics of Political De-regulation	Economics 511
Condom Etiquette for the 1990's	Public Health 201
Rape Defense Tactics Against Celebrity Males	Physical Ed. 310
Strategies of the Great Plains Chiefs	History 406
Advanced Deficit Forecasting	Mathematics 508
De-Constructionist Techniques of the Stoics (directed study)	Philosophy 705
Endangered Muskrat Habitats	Biology 420
Multi-Cultural Themes in 18th Century Criticism	English 601
Urban Chicano Muralism	Art History 507

14

Politically Incorrect Bestsellers

Americans have flocked into the bookstores and made many interesting titles bestsellers. But Politically Incorrect persons like ourselves aren't influenced by reviews or sales figures. We know a good read when we see one. Just give us the stuff the National Enquirer isn't brave enough to publish, especially if it is consistent with our collective bias.

Exposing JFK by Geraldo Rivera

Geraldo's video-taped investigation reveals that John F. Kennedy faked his own assassination and Marilyn Monroe's death. The couple secretly resides in a seaside villa in Ecuador enjoying a *menage à trois* with Elvis Presley.

Women Who Hate Men and the Men Who Love It by Mike Tyson

Former boxing champ theorizes on what makes women want it AND want to call it rape afterwards. Foreword by William Kennedy Smith.

The Art of the Steal by Donald Trump

Trump details his unorthodox strategies on how to look and act richer than you are, fool bankers and get them to loan you whopping sums for megalomaniac ventures, then declare bankruptcy so you can keep the bucks you couldn't earn yourself.

Addicted to Self-Destruction by Marion Barry

The disgraced mayor of Washington D.C. offers his techniques on dodging FBI sting operations and advocates survivalist training for Black politicians.

Everything I Need to Know I Learned from John Sununu by George Bush

A delightful compendium of philosophical conversations between Bush and his much misunderstood chief of staff. Smooth reading, great for bathroom engagements.

How to Make a Fortune Selling Toilet Paper by Michael Milken

The jailed junk bond artist explains how worthless paper can be salvaged and sold by simply printing official looking numbers on it.

Frommer's Guide to the Lower East Side

Now you too can traverse the hooker and homeless infested streets of New York's most politically incorrect neighborhood. Features illustrated and walking maps with authentic odors.

How to Pick Up Girls Who Really Want It by Clarence Thomas

Justice Thomas "exposes" his well-tested techniques for seducing women with long legs and graduate degrees.

The Movable Earthquake by Oprah Winfrey

Talk show hostess Winfrey shares her ups and downs leading a jogging tour of Swiss chocolate factories.

Oedipus Complex Gone Bad: The Untold Story of Saddam Hussein by Arthur "The Scud Stud" Kent

The star NBC reporter reveals that Saddam's obsession with "the mother of all wars" drove him crazy, and compelled him to invade Kuwait to rape Filipino housekeepers.

Thanks to God by Jim Bakker

Defrocked televangelist Bakker confesses the entire PTL scam was his grand plan to dump Tammy Faye.

Co-Defendant No More by General Manuel Noriega

The deposed Panamanian strongman admits to indiscretions but blames the CIA and DEA for tempting him. Lays blame for BCCI scandal squarely on the shoulders of Israel's super-secret Mossad.

American Psycho-Analyst by Brett Easton Ellis

Literary bad-boy Ellis apologizes for his depressing and misogynistic prose and blames it all on a Bennington education.

Room without a View by Leona Helmsley

Jailed dragon lady hotelier muses on the Ides of April while complaining about prison life and fashion.

15

Top Ten Politically Incorrect Christmas Gifts

The Holiday Season is as good a time as any to give our friends and admired ones gifts only we could enjoy. To guide you we have selected the top ten items every Politically Incorrect person can enjoy.

10. A tugboat to return refugees to Haiti.
9. Ted Kennedy swizzle sticks.
8. A Gennifer Flowers blow-up doll.
7. A Japanese car assembled in a former Brazilian rainforest.
6. David Duke for President campaign buttons and bumper stickers.

5. A southern-state Congressman.

4. A credit card from the House Bank.

3. Long Dong Silver candle stick holders.

2. A subscription to radio talk show host Rush Limbaugh's newsletter.

The #1 Politically Incorrect Christmas Gift:

1. A lifetime membership in the N.R.A.

16

PC Marketeering

Ever anxious to jump on one or another bandwagon, if for no other reason than to irk conservatives, PC-types quickly championed the case for safe sex because of the AIDS virus. Not wishing to appear prudish for fear of denigrating the relevance of their 1960'ish coming of age experiences, they invented enticing new contraceptive brand names to encourage men to wear condoms. Here are some they considered marketing:

BRAND NAME	SPECIAL FEATURES
Plough Boy	Country comfort, scented.
Ramrods	10W40 lubrication.

Pole Caps	Artificially chilled to prolong erection.
NBA Longs	Condoms for long and tall brothers.
Joe Meat's	Inexpensive and extra strong.
Heavy Hitter	Bigger sizes, enlarged sperm reservoir.
Iron Mike Brand	Extra tough and easy to remove.
Chili Con Carne	Flavored with or without onions; Spanish language instructions on packaging.

PC Marketeering...

17

Politically Incorrect One-Liners

—A perfect example of minority rule is a baby in the house.

—You can always spot a well-informed man. His views invariably coincide with yours.

—The politicians' promises of yesterday are the new taxes of today.

—A businessman who feels like he's going around in circles has probably cut too many corners.

—When a woman suffers in silence it usually means the telephone is out of order.

—The weird thing about trouble is that it often starts out being fun.

—If the PC name for history is *herstory* does that mean the PC term for Hell is *She'll?*

—If an appendectomy is the surgical removal of the appendix, and a tonsilectomy is the removal of the tonsils, is a dichotomy the firing of all PC feminist college professors from the faculty?

—Architects cover their mistakes with ivy, landscapers cover theirs with sod. PCers cover their mistakes with BS.

—Why do ACLU legal eagles always appeal cases where justice has been done?

—There's nothing worse than arguing with a person who know's what he's talking about!

—A woman who wants to talk about her inner feelings means she's pissed at you.

—Ethnic sensitivities have become so inflamed that it might be a hate crime to send back the egg rolls at a Chinese restaurant.

—Why do gays and lesbians feel compelled to walk in parades?

18

PC Acronyms

Marketing special interest organizations is a PC-advocate's speciality. Ever since the NAACP sprang forth to wave the banner of civil rights, they've been helping public and private groups organize to get their messages heard. We all know that finding a catchy name is the first rule for any publicity campaign. Here are a few organizations' acronyms and full names. See if you think they match appropriately.

ORGANIZATION ACRONYM	ORGANIZATION NAME
A.M.E.N.	American Men Endangered by Narcissism

ORGANIZATION ACRONYM	ORGANIZATION NAME
B.U.F.F.	Bisexuals United For Fun
C.H.M.A.G.	Communities Hopping Mad Against Gangs
C.R.U.D.	Committee to Re-vamp the Untenable Dictionary
F.A.R.T.S.	Feminists Against Racism, Tokenism and Sexism

ORGANIZATION ACRONYM	ORGANIZATION NAME
H.O.O.P.S.	Hands Off Our Parks Shithead
I.M.P.S.	International Multi-cultural Poets Society
N.U.D.I.E.	Nudists United to Drive Introverts into Extroversion
P.I.S.S.	Parent Interested in Safe Sex
P.O.C.O.	People Of Color Organized
P.U.T.Z.	People United to Trash all Zoos
S.O.T.S.	Save Our Threatened Species
W.A.C.K.O.S.	Women's Action Committee to Kill Off Sexists

19

Politically Incorrect Ways to Balance The U.S. Budget

When it comes right down to it, there are only four ways to reduce the whopping U.S. budget deficit: cut spending, raise taxes, sell off lease Federal assets or nationalize private property for public use. (You will note we have excluded the adoption of misleading accounting techniques from our list.) Since nobody seems willing to come forward and make the necessary hard choices, we assumed the responsibility for offering a few ideas:

—NATIONALIZE ALL PRO SPORTS TEAMS: Just think of the bucks the national treasury will reap by getting all those multi-year/multi-

million dollar contracts. And with public financing to raise funds for stadiums, we'll have even less overhead. What a scam!
Estimated Annual Take: $10–14 billion.

—INSTITUTE A THERAPY TAX: With the propensity of Americans to seek therapy for a myriad of real or imagined emotional and behavioral ailments, we could raise money AND feel great doing it. How perfectly painless!
Estimated Annual Revenue: $3–5 billion.

—CUT SOCIAL SECURITY PAYMENTS TO RICH SENIORS: Older Americans are by far the wealthiest Americans, yet they receive over $120 billion a year in handouts. Sure, many have paid into the system, but the arithmetic doesn't add up. More importantly, a full one-third are so rich they just don't need it.
Estimated Annual Savings: $40–50 billion.

—LEASE ALL CLOSED MILITARY BASES TO AMUSEMENT PARK OPERATORS: We saved a ton by closing down obsolete bases. Since this left a lot of communities at a loss, this proposal would be a fun and exciting way of bringing jobs back to town. By renting old fighter jets and nuclear subs for weekend recreation, we could raise even more.
Estimated Annual Revenue: $9–12 billion.

—NATIONALIZE COKE AND PEPSI: America's two giant soda pop manufacturers account for tens of billions in annual sales. We could merge them together (since nobody not on TV can tell the two apart) and create a single U.S. Cola, thereby monopolizing the industry. We'd sell oceans full!
Estimated Annual Sales: $16–19 billion.

—TAX CELEBRITY ENDORSEMENT FEES: We were shocked to learn how much sports stars and entertainers make from pitching products. Let's slap a 50 percent tax on their earnings, they won't feel it. And besides, maybe we'll be spared the indignity of watching Cher and Telly Savalas a dozen times a day. That's worth a bundle in itself! Estimated Annual Revenue: $2–3 billion.

—ABOLISH CONGRESS: We'll confess this isn't a novel idea, as others have proposed it for decades. It would go a long way in solving the deficit problem for good. We think the time for such action has finally arrived. Not only would we save the bundle it cost to staff and operate the place, we'd save billions annually by ending pork-barrel spending. And we could rent out the Capitol as a nightclub! Estimated Annual Savings: $25–150 billion

20

The New PC Criminal Code

People are getting so touchy about things we used to take for granted. Now we're supposed to be feeling guilty about them. If the PCers have their way, we might be found guilty of creating any number of the following:

—**ABLEISM:** Actions or remarks which reveal a prejudice against a person's physical abilities or inabilities, whatever the case.

—**AGEISM:** Actions or remarks which reveal a prejudice against a person's age, irrespective of maturity or lack thereof.

—**CLASSISM:** Prejudice based upon a person's or peoples' social and/or economic class, especially if those people receive government checks monthly.

—**ELITISM:** Wrongly thinking or presuming you are part of a privileged society if it entails excluding others (no matter their diseases or disabilities).

—**EUROCENTRISM:** Bias toward anything having to do with Europe, European heritage, culture, traditions and especially, European notions of democracy.

—**JINGOISM:** Actions or attitudes based upon a person's ethnic background, unless of course, they're Polish.

—**LOOKISM:** Prejudice against how a person looks or dresses. Not applicable to expensive restaurants and trendy discos.

—**VEHICLEISM:** Prejudice against what kind of vehicle one chooses to buy or drive, especially if it's an import.

21

Politically Incorrect Lectures

Universities, ever the champions of Political Correctness, have made a habit of sponsoring lectures by their leaders. It's about time we start doing the same. We especially want to emulate their ability to close their minds and open their wallets. Here are some suggested topics:

"How To Profit At The Expense Of The U.S. Government" by Jim Wright

"Writing a Tell-All Political Biography That Really Tells Nothing" by Donald Regan

"How To Handle Yourself Upon Indictment By A Special Prosecutor" by John Poindexter

"How I Grabbed The Presidency For 15 Minutes" by Al Haig

"Power Lunching The Ivan Boesky Way" by Ivan Boesky himself.

"Advanced Whining For Women With Balls" by Jeanne Kirkpatrick

"Know Your Enemies So You Can Destroy Them" by Gen. Norman Schwarzkopf and Gen. Colin Powell

"Married To A PC Junkie: A Survivor's Course" by Charlton Heston

"Did Fawn Hall Go South On North and Other Unanswered Questions From The Iran-Contra Affair" by Richard Secord (U.S. Army Ret.)

"How The U.S. Government Is Controlled By Latent Leninists And Ralph Nader Devotees" by Lyndon Larouche

"How To Spot Sexual Harassment Complainants At The Interview Stage" by Brock Adams (late of the U.S. Senate)

"Big City Mayors: True Causes Of The Homeless Problem In America" by Jack Kemp

22

PC Campaign Slogans

It's no wonder PC-speak and think reared its distasteful head in an election year. It's proponents will exploit any opportunity to influence otherwise politically innocent Americans. Here are a few of the more outrageous campaign slogans they attempted to get the major party candidates to adopt.

"Make all contributions to Latin American leftist groups tax deductible."

"Get the F.B.I. out of the hair of corrupt black mayors."

"Migrant farm workers deserve equal rights."

"Western oriented cultures are the primary cause for many of the world's ills."

"Conservative ideology is undermining diversity of opinion."

"Children from broken homes have a right to a government voucher good for one Ivy League university degree."

"No capital gains tax for the rich; end trickle-down theories."

"Buy American (unless of course you're shopping for a sports car)."

"Free therapy for introspective Americans."

"Tax credits for adopting homeless crack addicts."

"National health care for animals too!"

23

Excerpts from Underprivileged Ricardo's Daily Diary

It was only a matter of time before someone came up with a Politically Correct rip-off of Ben Franklin's POOR RICHARD'S ALMANAC. We managed to get a hold of several unpublished entries:

A penny saved . . . is one less going to the oppressed Third World masses.

Early to bed, early to rise, makes a man healthy, wealthy, and wise . . . and thus unworthy of any consideration, except to redistribute his wealth to national health care, to turn him down from the college of his choice, and re-educate him.

A bird in the hand . . . usually means that the bird is soaked in oil and pollution from man's defilement of Mother Earth.

An idle mind . . . makes one "mentally challenged" and eligible for affirmative action, parking spaces, entitlements, and anything except prosecution.

Never look a gift horse in the mouth . . . he might take it as insensitive and spit on you for being the species chauvanist you are!

There's a fox in the hen house . . . which is better than a man in the hen house!

An apple a day . . . keeps the doctor coming because it's coated with that horrible compound Alar. AAAUGHH!!

Sweet sixteen and never been kissed . . . a good thing, too, as kissing is just a kinder, gentler form of sexist objectification.

Waste not, want not . . . that's an order, not a choice!

He who laughs last . . . needs a fair shake. Broadcast all jokes on megaphones from every lamppost in the nation, and make everyone get lobotomies to insure that all humor is heard and understood by everyone at the same time.

The PC Golden Rule for Straight-White-European Males is . . . "Have others do unto you what your ancestors have done to theirs."

The PC Golden Rule for everyone else is . . . "Do unto others, then claim it's not your fault, but that a legacy of racism, sexism, homophobia, or any sociological force beyond your control."

24

Politically Incorrect Products

Astute manufacturers, obviously conservatives, have sensed the need—and the market—for Politically Incorrect products for us to use and enjoy. Here are a few samples from the latest editions of their catalogs:

PEST-AWAY LIBERAL REPELLANT: One squirt does the trick.

FINAL NET EXIT: Radioactive hairspray guaranteed to hold for life.

SPOT REMOVE-ALL: The fastest way to get rid of your neighbor's pesky dog.

SLIM-FASTER: For today's anorexics who just can't lose weight quick enough.

SLASH & BURN: A drop of this amazing ointment wipes out hundreds of acres of tropical rain forest for industrial development.

WINDCRUDDER: Beautiful 55-foot luxury yacht that doubles as a recycling barge fuel generator. Inexpensive to operate.

PHUNDUMS: Make her think you're responsible. Phundums melt on contact, allowing you to enjoy the experience without encountering her feelings of guilt.

COVER-UP GIRL: A new line of cosmetics for today's active CIA operative.

12-STEP MASTER: Exciting new exerciser for struggling alcoholics.

DOG-EAT-DOG FOOD: Offers man's best friend nutrition and street smarts.

SALVADORAN FRUIT JUICE SPRITZER: The delicious product of a neo-capitalist joint venture which employs thousands of former communist insurgents.

25

Unanswered Questions on the Clarence Thomas Confirmation Hearings

The Senate Judiciary Committee hearings on the Clarence Thomas Supreme Court nomination brought out all manner of Political Correctness in broods. The nationally broadcast spectacle proved to be a stimulating affair. Yet, after it was all over, we couldn't help but wonder what all the fuss was about. Despite the facts and allegations which were disclosed, many questions remain . . .

Will Pepsi use the transcripts to discredit Coca Cola or will it adopt the slogan, "You've got the politically correct one, baby! Uh, huh?"

Will love doctor Leo Buscalia get his license revoked for all that hugging?

Will women managers, as a response to "the glass ceiling," put their male co-workers in glass cubicles?

Will it come out that Senator Paul Simon is the long lost twin brother of popcorn maven Orville Reddenbacher?

Will Long Dong Silver shoot up or fall limp . . . in popularity, that is?

Will Senator Howell Heflin of Alabama ever learn to speak English?

Will the next nominee to the Supreme Court be forced to disclose suffering from hemorrhoids on national television?

Will South Carolina Senator (and state fossil) Strom Thurmond finally retire and go home to Brooklyn, where he sounds like he came from?

Will the Japanese buy out the American market for "high-tech lynching?"

Will Senator Edward Kennedy ("The Chappaquidick Kid") be offered the role of Pruneface whenever Warren Beatty makes DICK TRACY II.

Will word get out to Utah's Orrin Hatch's country club buddies that he and Israeli hawk Benjamin Netanyahu were separated at birth?

Lastly, will Anita Hill's new boyfriend receive a commendation from N.O.W?

26

Politically Incorrect Miscellany

—One good thing about PC is that such thinking, if fully adopted, will solve the abortion issue to everyone's satisfaction. After all, why argue over whether abortion is murder when we can simply conclude that all sex is exploitation, thus we wouldn't have any fetuses to argue about.

—The perfect gift for the PC Person is a box of air with nothing in it except a card saying, "Well, hell! If objective reality is a Western White Male Bourgeois prejudice, why are you expecting something to be in this box? Deconstruct this, smarty-pants."

—Those who speak of "consciousness-raising" need a little of their own medicine.

—Ain't it a mixed up world when any suffix -IN stands for an attempt to keep or kick someone OUT (for example, "sit-in," etc.), yet "outing" means getting "into" someone's private life.

—Now that the divestment campaign against South Africa's White su- premacist political regime seems to have borne fruit, what else will the PCers of the world have American business and institutions di- vest from?

—When will criminologists, big city mayors, defense attorneys and die- hard liberals understand that their "It's not your fault theory of crime," is largely responsible for the violent nature of American city streets.

—What is frequently referred to as "The Academic Canon" didn't have a name when we were going to college.

—Political Correctness is not so much something being advocated by liberals as it is something that is being attacked by conservatives. NOT!

—College speech codes opposing censorship are in fact censorship-motivated since the only things that can be addressed in an appropriate college forum must be PC.

—Liberals are quick to call upon their sympathizers in the entertainment industry to stage benefit concerts like FARM AID and FOOD AID. The Politically Incorrect among us should follow suit. We could organize WASP AID and HARASS AID, among others.

27

PC Rules of Academia

The standard rule of academia is "Publish or Perish." With the competition for our hearts and minds (and sympathies), PC do-gooders have posited their own definitions of academia:

Marxist Rule of Academia: Publish AND Perish!

Feminist Rule of Academia: Publish, and in so doing, try to bring down as many male writers as you can.

Afrocentric Rule of Academia: Publish? We wrote the book on publishing! How dare you steal our sacred institution!

Deconstructionist Rule of Academia: Publish or perish, but not necessarily in that order.

Hispanic Rule of Academia: We would have published a lot more if we weren't dominated by Anglo-European notions of educational policy.

Homosexual Rule of Academia: We were born to publish sexually explicit material.

Radical Liberal Rule of Academia: We shall publish so that we may undermine and/or revise the core curriculum of the university establishment.

28

Politically Correct Musicals and Plays

Before you spend money on season tickets, make sure you don't waste it on these future Politically Correct flops of stage and screen.

A Party Line—The Deconstructionist, Femi-Nazi version of *A Chorus Line* featuring the song: "One sin-gu-lar sen-sa-tion every goose-step she takes . . ."

Less Miserable—The PC distortion of *Les Miserables,* in which Victor Hugo's entire storyline gets destroyed when Jean Valjean gets off the hook and Jalvert becomes Valjean's caseworker instead of a detective.

The Social Worker—The PC blind swat at William Gibson's *The Miracle Worker* in which a PC Annie Sullivan comes to Helen Keller's home hell-bent on doing some social engineering. Instead of teaching Helen to sign, speak, and be a self-reliant human being, Sullivan gets Helen public assistance and teaches her to play a mean pinball.

Objectified Woman and the Animal Companion—The PC mutation of *Beauty and the Beast,* in which Beauty changes into an animal upon kissing her love. *Objectified . . .* gets two thumbs up from both the 'animal rights' movement and radical feminists who emulate shaggy females.

The Princess and the PC—The PC play about a PC queen who finds a PC princess for the PC prince. To win her sweetheart the princess must sleep on twenty mattresses with a *Playboy* on the bottom. The sensitivity of the princess to the sexist literature keeps her awake and thus makes her a true PC princess who gets the man and wins a rare PC happy ever after.

Dead Enemy of the People—The PC version of Henrik Ibsen's *Enemy of the People* in which the mob prevails over the genius Dr. Stockmann.

A GI-Joe's House—Robert Bly version of Henrik Ibsen's *A Doll's House* in which the *husband* walks out in the climactic end scene.

The Crushable—The PC biodegrading of Arthur Miller's play *The Crucible* where Salem Puritans burn little girls at the stake for using unrecyclable drink boxes.

Man of de Man-cha—A Deconstructionist distortion of Cervantes' *Don Quixote* in which windmills really are dragons, since Quixote's "intentionality" dictates that they are.

29

The New PC Men's Movement

Our continued focus on the national women's movement has over-shadowed a corresponding rise of a men's movement across America. Prompted principally by the perceived inequality of divorce courts in granting them custody of their minor children, even in cases of gross maternal incompetence, men have now become keenly aware of their vanishing power and masculinity. To try and exorcise their feelings of impotence, men across the nation have organized so-called Sweat Lodges, super secret male-only retreats where the meaning of manhood is revealed to participants. Listed below are some of the more popular sweat lodges and descriptions of their attractions.

SWEAT LODGE NAME	ITS MAJOR ATTRACTIONS
Buck's Dude Ranch	Gambling parlor, topless waitresses and complimentary adult videos. Fish-fry all-you-can-eat reception Fridays.
Tom Tom Club	Drum beating instruction, loin-cloth design course; a "howling" good time promised.
Iron John's Retreat	Ideal for sensitive, literate types; free beer and tortillas all weekend.
Camp Al Bundy	Emphasizes feeling pride in laziness, learning to veg out without guilt; talk about women prohibited; sports talk encouraged.

SWEAT LODGE NAME	ITS MAJOR ATTRACTIONS
The Tool School	Teaches alternate uses for the penis; rape charge denial techniques. Offers one-half off for blood brothers.
Muscle Head Creek	Male bonding taught; features growling contests, mud-wrestling; fun for all.
Dave and Ed's	The Ben and Jerry of sweat lodges, D & E's offers cabins with locker room aromas, hole-in-the-wall urinals and lots of space to throw your dirty clothes around.
The Treehouse	"Be A Boy Again" play-acting; stick whittling, puddle diving; Nintendo war games instructions.
Wildman Weekends	Tarzan's law of the jungle explained; plenty of time for tree swinging, coconut hunting and other "outdoor" recreations.

30

Politically Incorrect Honeymoon Packages

So you've tied the Politically Incorrect knot for life and are ready for that special honeymoon to inspire the both of you. Forget traditional destinations like Acapulco or Hawaii. They're hotbeds of unionist unrest. Try these packages to get you where you want to be:

Club Chernobyl

At Club Chernobyl and Chernobyl Spas you'll never have a problem getting a tan, though we advise you to use SPF #1000 skin block to achieve that special "Plutonium Bronze." Out of work Soviet nuclear scientists cater to your every whim. Lovers of Steve Lawrence and

Eydie Gormet will enjoy Mike and Raisa singing their top hits "What We Doobie-Do Now," and "What's the Matter with Reds Today?"

Poachman's African Safaris

Feast at our All-You-Can-Eat Endangered Species Buffet! You may never get a chance to sample these tasty animals again. Hunt elephants from the comfort of air-conditioned Mercedes 4-wheelers, while you sip Martinis served by dollar-a-day valets. Special discounts if you surrender your ivory at the border. Book fast, supplies are dwindling.

God's Garden Colombia

The Medellin Cartel welcomes you and sponsors your entire honeymoon—free! Enjoy a breathtaking view of street riots from the presidential suite at the Bogata Hilton. Sunbathe in fashionable Cartagena. Explore the jungles of the interior. All you have to do is agree to deliver a relatively compact piece of luggage to one of our representatives at Miami International Airport. Deluxe complimentary packages available for U.S. diplomats.

The China Nobody Knows

Meet Asian celebrities when you visit the set of China's hottest television game show, Tienanmen Squares. Dine and dance on a sumptuous Yangtse riverboat dinner cruise. Stroll leisurely along the Great Wall and see students throw Molotov cocktails. Side packages available to Tibet, Hong Kong, and the Gobi Desert. Hurry, exchange rates are slowing down.

Saddam's Iraqi Adventure

Visit war-ravaged Baghdad and see Cruise missile bomb craters. Iraqi zoo features Iranian prisoners of war, Kuwaiti sheiks and U.N. weapons detection specialists. Get in the mood by watching our 24-hour cable television channel featuring taped confessions of captured American pilots. Food is scarce so expect to lose weight. Deep discounts for knowledgeable nuclear scientists.

31

PC Daytime Talk Show Topics

The television has long been criticized as a purveyor of smut and slime. Yet, it could probably make an arguable case for being a reflection of our society, which is a lot of both. Daytime talk shows like DONAHUE, OPRAH, GERALDO and their clones have done an excellent job of keeping this sad fact foremost in our minds. Of course, they're quintessentially PC presentations:

The Sins of Our Fathers: An odd slew of troubled youngsters blame their fathers, and uncles in a few cases, of verbally abusing them by calling them bums, idiots and the like. Not unexpectedly, the entire lot of them look to be exactly that.

The Sins of Our Founding Fathers: Feminists, blacks and socialist professors blame the nation's founding fathers for their sins. From the level and frequency of their accusations, you'd think they were a bunch of losers.

The Polygamous Extended Family: Utah family professes the joy of free-love, nepotism and family nights at Pizza Hut.

Senior Citizens Bankrupted by Protestant S&L Executives: America's grandpas and grandmas denounce Reaganesque excesses, call session "therapeutic."

Family Counselors Who Advocate Incest: Leading psychologists explain the virtues of incest in a "respectful, loving atmosphere."

Why the Ten Commandments Are Wrong: Revisionist theologians suggest Moses may have altered tablets to foster male-dominated attitudes.

Spouses Who Love Union Members: Union family members discuss the pros and cons of membership, benefits and unemployment activities.

Rap Singers Who Curse Excessively: Citing rap as the most vital form of communication to America's underclass, rappers share their views on the purpose of swearing in their lyrics.

Mothers-in-Law Who Hate Themselves: The trials and tribulations of mother-in-lawdom are discussed by women who have attempted suicide over the loss of their "Little Ones."

Depraved Sex Education Counselors: Torrid tales of teacher misconduct reveal the true cause of teenage sexual dysfunctionalism.

Modern Mainstream Dropouts: Guests explain why they gave up their families and careers in search of their dreams of self-fulfillment.

Educators for Fast Track Cultural Diversity: Prominent educators express their beliefs that cultural diversity in classrooms is lagging behind sex-ed in popularity.

32

Our Parents As Culprits

Children of any generation can blame their parents for any number of faults and omissions in their lifetimes. One wonders what the efficacy of such fault-finding can be. Despite this, a number of prominent people, Latoya Jackson, Roseanne Barr-Arnold, Suzanne Somers and Patti Davis (Reagan) among them, have chosen to exorcise their pasts by laying the blame for their troubles squarely on the shoulders of their fathers. If this was universally practiced, it could lead to some bizarre allegations.

George Washington could blame his father or mother (maybe both) for his premature graying, Abraham Lincoln could blame his parents for his awkward figure and Franklin D. Roosevelt could blame his parents for giving him polio.

Napoleon might have been a peaceable chap if he couldn't blame his height on his father or his mother for his inferiority complex. Lizzy Borden may have been a model daughter if her parents hadn't driven her crazy enough to butcher them with an axe. Leon Czolgosz, the man who assassinated President William McKinley, would have probably never become an anarchist if his father had let him milk the family cow.

Libyan leader Muammar Kaddafi might have been a world renowned fashion designer if his mother would have encouraged him to play with dolls instead of toy soldiers. Adolf Hitler might have been a great architect if his parents would have paid for his education in Vienna. Josef Stalin might have been an Orthodox priest if his mother hadn't force-fed him the Bible.

Susan B. Anthony could have lived a happy life as a school marm if her father let her wear slacks. Lech Walesa could have been another hack electrician if he didn't have parents who insulted his intelligence and belittled his accomplishments. Nelson Mandela could have been a champion boxer if his father let him poach chickens from white farmers.

33

You Gotta Believe Quiz

To be Politically Incorrect you must have a core of strongly held beliefs. Whether your beliefs have any factual basis is irrelevant; the important thing is your level of adherence. The following true-false quiz has been designed to determine the strength of your Politically Incorrect views. Remember, your answers should reflect what you firmly believe, not whether the statement is accurate.

TRUE   FALSE
1. _____ _____ Ronald Reagan was the greatest U.S. President since Abraham Lincoln.

2. _____ _____ The problem with George Bush is he talks like a conservative but acts like a moderate.

3. _____ _____ A capital gains tax cut, deregulation, hostile takeovers and leveraged buyouts with junk bond financing are the keys to a prosperous economy.

4. _____ _____ Women don't want and don't need careers outside the home.

5. _____ _____ Blacks and Hispanics have no ambition and actually enjoy doing menial labor for the minimum wage.

6. _____ _____ The Democratic-controlled Congress is solely to blame for the federal budget deficit.

7. _____ _____ Unions are largely responsible for the decline of American industrial might.

8. _____ _____ Juvenile delinquency can be traced to the abolishment of school prayer.

9. _____ _____ Sex education has led to the increase in teenage pregnancies.

10. _____ _____ If someone is unemployed, even if its your own child, it's their own damned fault.

11. _____ _____ Welfare and other government handouts have destroyed the American work ethic.

12. _____ _____ Abortion is murder, no doubt about it!

13. _____ _____ Clarence Thomas told the truth and Anita Hill lied.

14. _____ _____ All of women's problems have been a consequence of feminist gains.

15. _____ _____ Global warming and ozone depletion are myths propagated by environmentalists.

16. _____ _____ Civil Rights laws lead directly to the establishment of hiring quotas.

17. _____ _____ Nuclear power is the safest and cleanest form of energy.

18. _____ _____ The U.S. government cannot afford national health insurance.

19. _____ _____ Family maternity leaves and mandated daycare will destroy the American family and the competitiveness of American industry.

20. _____ _____ Star Wars technology is essential even without a Russian nuclear threat.

21. _____ _____ AIDS is God's punishment for homosexuality.

22. _____ _____ A fetus, being unprotected, should always have more rights than the mother.

23. _____ _____ The lack of affordable housing has nothing whatsoever to do with homelessness.

24. _____ _____ The death penalty is the single best deterrent to serious crime.

25. _____ _____ This book ought to be required reading in university classes across the nation.

Score five points for each True answer and zero points for each False answer.

If your score is 50 or lower, then you're one of those liberals who likes to be politically correct at all times. Worse than that, you also like to verify facts.

If your score is from 55–85, then you're a weenie who doesn't worry about political correctness but who prefers to base your beliefs on conventional wisdom.

If your score is 90 or higher, then you are gloriously Politically Incorrect. You've shown that the truth won't get in the way of what you ardently believe. Accolades are in order.

Politically Correct Shakespeare

The Politically Correct aren't just out to "rehabilitate" Western history, but also have it in for Western literature . . . starting with none other than the Bard himself. Here's what you can expect from the psychobabblers of soul, sisterhood, sissyness and sychophancy:

Politically Correct *Macbeth*

". . . Is this a phallic domineering, male dagger I see before me, or is it but a deconstructionist dagger of the mind?"

". . . Life's but a National Endowment of the Arts-funded actor, an underprivileged player/ That performs his bathroom functions during his hour upon the stage/ And then dies of STDs; it is a tale/ Told by one of the 'mentally-challenged,' full of revisionist history,/ Signifying an 'alternate lifestyle.'"

Politically Correct *Romeo and Juliet*

"But soft, what bricks through yonder animal lab window fly?/ It is East, and and fair Juliet is the Sun Goddess! . . ."

"Oh Romeo! Romeo! Wherefor art thou, Romeo, thou typical dance-away male./ Blame thy father and affirm thy 'ethnic identity.'"

Politically Correct *Much Ado About Nothing*

"The lady doth not protesteth enough!"

Politically Correct *King Lear*

"An 'Equine Victim of Speciesism!'
An 'Equine Victim of Speciesism!'
My Kingdom for an 'Equine Victim of Speciesism!'"

35

Politically Correct 'Syndromes'

At one time, people in the Western World considered certain acts cool or faddish, tactful or boorish, neat or gross, wise or stupid, safe or dangerous, even good or evil. To judge human actions this way presupposes and implies recognition that man has free will and individual responsibility for his actions. The Political Correctness horde, however, rejects these basic facts of human nature as Western prejudice. Instead, the Politically Correct say that every human action results from some 'dysfunction' or, to be exact, some 'syndrome' outside man's control, yet somehow 'curable' with federal funds, 'rehabilitation' programs, and the latest 12-step cult. Here are some examples of what ugly behavior the Politically Correct would turn into a 'syndrome' if given the chance.

Nail-biting would become 'Dental Digital Protein Removal and Consumption Syndrome.'

Nose-picking would become 'Digital Nasal Mucous Membrane Removal and Consumption Syndrome.'

Teeth-gritting would become 'Inter-Dental Organic Material Removal and Display Syndrome.'

Cutesy names among couples would become 'Inter-Significant Other Neonymity Syndrome.'

Toe-jam picking would become 'Inter-Phlangal Fibrous Material Removal Obsession Syndrome.'

Naval lint-picking would become 'Umbilical Cavity Fibrous Material Removal Obsession Syndrome.'

Nymphomania would become 'Feminine Self-Objectification Syndrome.'

Breach of trust would become 'Lingual-Performance Discrepancy Syndrome.'

Rape would become 'Compulsory Coitus Syndrome.'

Cannibalism would become 'Aboriginal Intra-Species Consumption Syndrome.'

and finally,

Murder would become 'Other-Directed Permanent Animation Removal
Syndrome.'

We're surprised that they haven't come up with 'Unnecessary Syndrome Creation Syndrome' and prescribed alum for the mouths of
those who have the syndrome.

36

Politically Correct Challenges

The Political Correctness horde has made it standard practice to make any deficiency or limit—whether chosen or unchosen, whether good, bad, or indifferent—into a 'challenge.' The handicapped are 'Physically-Challenged' or 'Mentally-Challenged,' the bankrupt are the 'Financially-Challenged,' and so on. This practice of the Politically Correct partially covers up their own deficiencies or pins the blame elsewhere. But more than anything, making limits into 'challenges' is simply an attempt to make something out of nothing.

Making something out of nothing was absurd 2,600 years ago when some Eastern shaman put it down on papyrus as an idea for creation of the world. It is equally absurd when the Politically Correct put it into practice by making a world in their own image within the firmament of their own skulls.

Here are some of the 'challenges' you may see in the future from the Politically Correct. We must warn the Politically Correct: you will look down upon them and they will not be good. You may want to take a whole week to recover from them. What was once:

A bored person . . . is now the 'Challenge-Challenged.'

A Willie Loman salesman . . . is now the 'Capitalistically-Challenged.'

A failure . . . is now the 'Achievementally-Challenged.'

A dead person . . . is now the 'Metabolically-Challenged.'

An impotent man . . . is now the 'Erectionally-Challenged.'

A frigid woman . . . is now the 'Erotically-Challenged.'

A repressed woman . . . is now the 'Expressionally-Challenged.'

An enslaved person . . . is now the 'Movementally-Challenged.'

A starving person . . . is now the 'Nutritionally-Challenged.'

"I've fallen and I can't get up!" . . . is now expressed as: "I've been 'Gravitationally-and Bipedally-Challenged.'"

A lazy person . . . is now the 'Motivationally-Challenged.' (Try saying that one after a fifth of V.O.)

A redneck . . . is now the 'Enlightenmentally-Challenged.'

A bald head . . . is now the 'Folliclely-Challenged.'

The Unemployed . . . are now the 'Occupationally-Challenged.'

A promiscuous person . . . is now the 'Scrupulously-Challenged.'

An Alcoholic . . . is now the 'Sobrietily-Challenged.'

A stupid person . . . is now the 'Sensibly-Challenged.'

Breathlessness . . . is now a state of being 'Respiratorily-Challenged.'

A toothless old man . . . is now called one of the 'Dentally-Challenged.'

A shameless hussy . . . is now one of the 'Regretfully-Challenged.'

A Gentile . . . is now called 'Hebraically-Challenged.' or perhaps 'Circumcisionally-Challenged.'

A flat-chested woman . . . is now 'Mammarily-Challenged.'

An addict . . . is now 'Substantially-Challenged.'

An amputee . . . is now 'Anatomically-Challenged.'

A limited-time offer . . . is now 'Eternally-Challenged.'

An expelled student . . . is now 'Scholastically-Challenged.'

Schlock . . . is now the 'Qualitatively-Challenged.'

A naked person . . . is 'Garmentally-Challenged.'

A bigot . . . is 'Tolerantly-Challenged.'

And finally, since everything that exists has limits of some kind, the Politically Correct, true to their nihilistic mindset, think that: *Everything is nothing if it isn't challenged.*

37

The Scouts and Political Correctness

The Boy Scouts of America, that venerable institution of American pride in youth, has recently taken a licking over its membership rules. Let's look at a few examples:

In Kalamazoo, Michigan, as in a number of locales around the nation, a local scout troop was widely ostracized for refusing to admit girls. Upon being told that Boy Scouts is for boys and Girl Scouts is for girls, the parents of the girls went to court to seek an injunction after being denied membership. At last sight they were still duking it out before a federal judge.

In Nevada City, California, the son of atheist parents was refused admission into his local Boy Scout troop because they objected to the membership pledge swearing affirmation to God. The scouts insisted rules were rules and refused to grant the boy an exemption. The parents promptly consulted the ACLU, which accepted the challenge. The case is expected to ultimately reach the U.S. Supreme Court for yet another Church vs. State ruling.

In Salem, Oregon, the parents of (another unfortunate) boy objected to hunting and tracking activities, claiming they taught boys "Survivalist" techniques which they claim are anti-social, anti-conservationist, and a dozen other wrong things. Rather than wreck the other boys enjoyment of such harmless instruction, the parents convinced their son to join their local Boy's Club instead.

In Priest Lake, Tennessee, a school teacher objected to a Boy Scout troop using the school for meetings because it banned girls. Rather than wage an expensive legal battle, the scouts agreed to meet in the troop leader's garage. That it's grossly unlit and unheated was apparently of no consequence to the self-righteous teacher.

Parents of Boy Scout Troop 311 in Springfield, Illinois raised quite a fuss after it was discovered that a troop leader was homosexual and may have inappropriately touched two youngsters. The state scout council immediately suspended the troop leader pending a police investigation. Gay and lesbian rights advocates jumped on the case as another example of homophobia hysteria. Criminal sexual conduct charges were filed against the former troop master. The ACLU was considering whether to handle the matter because, as a spokesman said, "Fondling which would be perfectly innocent by a heterosexual male is in jeopardy of being labeled criminal if done by a homosexual male." One wonders when "fondling" of any kind was perfectly innocent when the "fondlee" is a 10 year-old.

38

New Age and the Politically Correct

At first, you would think that the Political Correctness horde simply contents itself with trashing that oppressive Western culture which brought us *Common Sense, The Age of Reason,* the Declaration of Independence, the Constitution, and the Bill of Rights (including the Civil War Amendments and the 19th Amendment.) This is sadly not the case. The Political Correctness horde also loves trashing the entire rational, secular, scientific worldview shared by Thomas Jefferson, James Madison, Thomas Paine and others who made Western culture's greatest achievements. Since Marxist dialectical materialism is going out of vogue as a replacement for this Western worldview, the Politically Correct now propose an idiotic collection of supernatural, wooly-bully, boogly-woogly bull called New Age philosophy.

New Age philosophy is best described as a household, a haunted household made from select rotting planks from the fungi-infested forests of Eastern mysticism. No one would buy it if it weren't made marketable with the Elmer Gantry-like snake-oil salesmanship prevalent in Middle Eastern-imported Western mysticism. Inside the household, there's the Bagwhan Shree Rajneesh and Elizabeth Claire Prophet as the grandparents, Ben Randall from Time-Life Books as the father, Shirley MacLaine as the mother, plus Lisa Bonet and John Travolta as older siblings. Each household member is very different, yet all have one thing in common: every move they make in their wretched lives serves another family member, a whiny, wimpy, bratty, baying, bawling, crying, crummy, *Christkindl* known by many names but mainly called the Inner Child. This delinquent Inner Child is really a hypochondriac 40-year old who thinks he is a psychosomatic free-bleeder. His family kow-tows to the Inner Child's neurosis and allows him to roam with no impediments of word or deed to scar him beyond repair, yet the Inner Child bears no responsibility for his own well-being.

A household where such mollycoddling takes place is a sure bed-and-breakfast for the Politically Correct who feel themselves to be victims of society who need some babying. Through the following set of one-liners, we want to serve as an intellectual Bob Vila and help you condemn this old New Age house, in hopes that the family might move to Tibet where they belong, that the Inner Child might get a place of his own, and above all, that the Politically Correct won't have a base of operations.

New Age Joke Sampler

Q: How do New Age women turn on New Age men?
A: They show them their jewels.

Did you hear about the New Age man with diaper rash? He forgot to change his Inner Child.

Q: What do Texas New Agers use as their mantra in Transcendental Meditation?
A: Ohm, Ohm on the range . . .

Q: What did George Bush say when Bhagwan Shree Rajneesh got caught by the authorities?
A: 'He's a guru in deep do-do!'

Q: What do you call a sexual encounter between New Agers?
A: A Harmonic Convergence.

Q: What's the New Age cause for the Nineties?
A: Inner Child Day Care.

Q: Which New Age perfume bottle contains the spirit of 'Ramtha'?
A: Channeler Number 5.

Did you hear about the lawsuit between two New Age women? One wanted to have custody of the other's surrogate Inner Child.

Q: What do New Agers say when they pass wind?
A: 'My Inner Child's having a temper tantrum.'

Did you hear about Gerber selling empty baby food jars? They said it was food for your Inner child.

Q: What is the New Age excuse for getting fat?
A: My Inner Child's just growing.

Did you hear about the New Age psychic travel agency? They have a special package tour to Shambala and a frequent out-of-body flyer plan.

Did you hear about the New Ager who was busted for drinking in the privacy of his own home? The charge: contributing to the delinquency of an Inner Minor.

Did you hear about the Karmaic toy store for Inner Children? It's called We 'R' Toys.

Q: What do racist New Agers say about interracial marriage?
A: Would you want *your* Inner Daughter to marry one?

A paper towel commercial has the slogan: 'The New Age of Cost Consciousness.' This is really just a kinder, gentler way of saying that the recession is making us all as poor as Hindus.

A New Age insult: Get Another Life!

New Age Technology and Political Correctness

You may still have questions about the link between Political Correctness and New Age philosophy. You may ask: 'What do Marxism, multiculturalism, revisionist history/herstory, and affirmative action have to do with contacting the spirit world?'

Aside from the fact that all these ideas are pretty loopy, they're all loopy in a particular way: they all seek somehow to change a dead past that can never be changed, they all ignore what presently lies before us as 'transitory', and they all aspire toward an impossible future which would be living Hell even if it were possible. Whether they try to change the past with seances or racial quotas or books like *Black Athena,* whether the transitory present is called 'this world' or 'the dictatorship of the Proletariat,' whether the impossible future is called 'Nirvana' or meeting the next timetable,' all the rest is a matter of detail.

Also, just as the Politically Correct condemn the West while gladly using Western freedom and Western technology, so also the New Agers do the same in their own way, through 'healing crystals' and L. Ron Hubbard's so-called E-meter.

In the fine Politically Incorrect capitalist tradition of 'let the buyer beware,' here's a forewarning of some of the hokey New Age technology for channelling spirits. You may find them at the nearest carrot juice bar, so be careful!

Satellite Dish Channelling—This is for the Inner Redneck who really wants to shake ol' Jim Beam's hand and find out if Heaven really is a lot like Dixie. Combined with a dual-screen Magnavox, you can find out the mystery of Bigfoot while watching the Bigfoot races on the Nashville Network. You can also find out if Hank Williams, Sr. is really proud of his younger same-named offspring, plus you can channel spirits of dead porn queens.

Cable-Channelling—With this, you can channel the basic dead spirits on Public TV, Premium dead spirits such as Spencer Tracy, Marilyn Monroe, and the braindead spirit Ronald Reagan on American Spook Classics, or the more contemporary *Ghosts* on Spiritmax, Spectertime, or the Amityville Home Box Office.

Pay-Per-Seance—This versatile feature of Cable Channelling enables you to see exclusive events such as concerts from dead rock-n-roller spirits Elvis Presley, Jimi Hendrix, and Janis Joplin. You can also see boxing matches among dead boxers such as Mighty Joe Young, although you'll still get De-Con commercials from the mentally-dead spirit of Muhammed Ali. You'll also get a glimpse of what otherworldly punishments await Mike Tyson.

Catbear Multi-Channel Scanners—This is for channelling police, fire, and ambulance spirits like Eliot Ness, Mrs. O'Leary, and Dorethea Dix respectively. The Catbear Multi-Channel Scanner keeps you on top of all the emergency events decades after everyone is dead and gone.

Programmable Multi-Channel Scanners—This is like the Catbear, only with a broader spectrum of spirit frequencies such as short-wave ham spirit Guglielmo Marconi, T.V. spirits Groucho Marx and Edward R. Murrow (and Murrow thought television was a 'vast wasteland!'), or even x-ray spirits like Wilhelm Roentgen. The Programmable Multi-Channel Scanner may displease some New Agers because no crystals are required, but all in all, it's a must for every New Age home.

Rabbit Ear Channelling—This is the most economical way to channel spirits. Unfortunately, all you can get are mentally-dead networks like Fox or dead re-run actors like Redd Foxx. This option offers the least channelling variety.

41

Ad Copy Excerpt from the Politically Correct Products and Services Catalog

Political Correct-All

Do you think you are a unique sovereign individual with the right to life, liberty, and the pursuit of happiness? Do you think you can achieve your dreams regardless of your race, gender, or color? Do you believe in the importance of the classics?

If so, then you suffer from constipation with the uptight values of Western Civilization. You need Political Correct-All!

Yes, Political Correct-All can help because it's fortified with alum, all-natural cyanide from wild apricot pits, LSD, Indian Pemmican, black draught and PMS hormones. It tightens up your mouth so insensitive speech is eliminated, numbs out the right brain's evil thoughts, induces race consciousness and purges your body politic of all anti-social elements.

Political Correct-All. We'll make a New Man or Woman out of you even if it kills you!

Rubberman Garbage Can

Members of the Sisterhood! Are you tired of using Politically Incorrect, non-biodegradable plastic garbage cans with sexist names like Rubbermaid?

Then try the Rubberman Garbage Can! It's made of biodegradable Peruvian rubber harvested by native proletarians working under the gentle hand of the Shining Path revolutionaries!

What's more, Rubberman Garbage Cans are shaped like men and are the ideal Femi-Nazi archetype of the male species! With the toughness of Iron John and the sensitivity of Alan Alda, it can take all the crap you throw at it! And since Rubberman Garbage Cans don't respond and all look alike, they'll confirm all your neuroses about how men are all scum and just don't listen!

Don't you wish every man was made like Rubberman?

The Deconstructionist Public Relations Firm, P.C.

Do you have Overloaded credit? Bad credit? No credit? Audits? Bankruptcy? Repossession? Foreclosure? Insurance Points? DWI? Drug and alcohol problems? Misdemeanor or felony charges? Or even crimes against humanity on your hands? No problem!

Turn to The Deconstructionist Public Relations Firm, P.C.

(That stands for Professional Corporation, Politically Correct, or Professed Crud, take your pick.)

We can help you get out of any problem you may have! With our "Big Lie" method, we can convince your employer, banker, creditor, insurer, psychologist, police, judges, parole officers, even the whole world, that *nothing* you've done is real!

We can even convince them that *nothing* is real if you like!

We operate on a special contingency fee (yes, we do get paid! You think we believe our own nonsense?) You don't pay unless we put one over on them!

Our satisfied clients include former House Speaker Jim Wright and Senator Ted Kennedy; former UN Secretary-General Kurt Waldheim; David Duke; Willis Carto; The Reverends Jesse Jackson, Robert Tilton, Al Sharpton, and Jim Bakker; Tawana Brawley, and more politicians and used-car salesmen than we can count! So call us today at 1-800-COW PIES, 1-800-NU-SPEAK, or 1-800-I'M A NAZI.

Heidegger and De Mann's Deconstructionist Window Cleaning Service

Tired of those smudged, dusty, dirty windows in your storefront? Want to avoid the environmentally unsafe practice of squirting them down with ammonia and other harmful chemicals?

Then call Heidegger and De Man's Deconstructionist Window Cleaning Service with experience going as far back as 1933, Window Cleaners Martin Heidegger and Paul De Man can solve your window cleaning problems forever.

Using their special, patented *Krystallnacht* method, Heidegger and De Man will smash your windows, then use existentialist, subjectivist literary philosophy and revisionist history mumbo-jumbo to convince you that your windows never got smashed and are bright and shiny as ever. These guys work so quietly, you won't even know they're there.

In fact, when it's all over, though you may not think to notice, *You won't even be there!*

Bonded and Licensed by American Academia.

Insured by the Kurt Waldheim Insurance Agency.

AND REMEMBER OUR SLOGAN:

We Have Ways of Making You Call!

42

PC and the Bible

If political correctness was around when the Bible was written the holy book might look something like this:

The New PC Ten Commandments

1. I am the Lord your God, although I'm not sure if I exist.
2. Thou shalt not pray in public school, profanity is okay.
3. Keep Holy Martin Luther King's Birthday or No Superbowl for you.

4. Honor Thy Father and Mother and then write an exposé on how you were an abused child.
5. Thou shalt not kill, except for fetuses.
6. Thou shalt commit adultery (extra points awarded for Nontraditional Partner Participants.)
7. Stealing is Okay if you earn below the federal poverty level.
8. Only liberal democrats can bear false witness against their neighbors.
9. Thou shalt not covet your neighbor's wife, unless she initiates the relationship.
10. Only the government has a right to covet your neighbor's goods, especially if he earns over $100,000. Thou shalt redistribute the wealth.

PC Sermon on the Mount

Happy are those who know they are not white, males of European descent; America will slowly be given to them.

Happy are those who live in prison; liberal lawmakers will get them maid service before the turn of the century.

Happy are those who are politically correct; they will receive an honorary membership to the National Organization of Women.

Happy are those who are African American descendants of the disenfranchised; for they will receive reparations.

Happy are the multiculturalists; they will dominate school curriculum.

Happy are gay rights activists; they will be recognized as the true sexual lifestyle.

Happy are the environmentalists; they will inherit the homeless.

Happy are the feminists; they shall see Geraldine Ferrarro.

Happy are those who criticize Reagan and Bush; theirs is the kingdom of socialism.

Happy are drug addicts, welfare puppies, looters, and societal misfits; they will receive government assistance.

THE OLD TEN COMMANDMENTS

43

Politically Incorrect Nursery Rhymes

Nursery Rhymes are usually the first stories that children encounter in the area of literature. PC'ers believe that no one is too young to become politically correct. If they get their way nursery rhymes that have remained unencumbered by revisionism may be drastically altered. Below are a few examples of how some old favorites might be changed.

BAA BAA MELANIN POSITIVE SHEEP

Baa, baa melanin positive sheep
have you any fake fur?

Yes, person, yes, person, three bags full.
One for my political oppressor,
one for my matriarch,
And one for the monetarily subjugated
people who live in the park.

THREE VISUALLY IMPAIRED MICE

Three visually impaired mice!
Three visually impaired mice.
See how they move! See how they move!
They were seen by the farmer's better half;
She nurtured and gave them a place on her staff.
And now no one should dare to laugh at
Three visually impaired mice.

THE LONG-LIVED FEMALE WHO LIVED IN A SHOE

There was a long-lived female
who lived in a shoe.
She had so many children
she didn't know what to do.
The government tried to cut
her claims for AFDC,
But she won in federal court,
and went on a shopping spree.

AGE CHALLENGED MOTHER HUBBARD

Age challenged female parent Hubbard
went to the cupboard, to get
her monetarily subjugated dog a bone,

but when she got there
The cupboard was bare,
and so the fiscally challenged canine had none.

CULTURALLY DENIED SIMON

Culturally Denied Simon met working girl Diane
On the way to get his AIDS test;
Says Culturally Denied Simon to working girl Diane
"Let me touch your breast."

Says working girl Diane to culturally denied Simon,
"Show me first twenty bucks."
Says Culturally Denied Simon to working girl Diane,
"I guess I'm out of luck."

44

PC & Baby Boom Music

Music of the 1950s and 1960s was radically different from the music of other decades. The songs of this era included hits by the Beatles, Jim Croce, Elvis, The Platters, etc. Many of the songs of this time period would make excellent theme songs for the many causes that are presently being rammed down the throats of the American public. Here are a few revised song titles and titles of existing songs that might accommodate themes of the PC organizations.

Existing Song Titles

"There Goes My Baby" originally performed by The Drifters. This would be the Pro Choice theme song.

"To Know Him Is To Love Him" originally performed by the Teddy Bears. This would be the official Act Up or Queer Nation theme song.

"You've Lost That Lovin' Feelin'" originally performed by the Righteous Brothers. This could be a dual anthem shared by those advocating public school condom distribution programs or for eunuch rights activists.

"Ain't No Mountain High Enough" originally performed by Diana Ross. The national anthem for women desiring breast implant surgery.

"Raindrops Keep Falling on My Head" originally performed by B.J. Thomas. This could be the song used to make people sorry for the homeless.

"I'm Sorry" originally performed by Brenda Lee. The song PC'ers would like played at the Republican National Convention.

"I Never Loved a Man" originally performed by Aretha Franklin. The Bill Clinton prepared theme alibi song for his next sex scandal.

"The Great Pretender" originally performed by the Platters. The historical revisionists ballad concerning textbook accounts of Columbus' discovery of North America.

"The Sun Ain't Gonna Shine Anymore" originally performed by the Walker Brothers. The global warming theme song.

Revised Song Titles

"Love My Gender," (Formerly, "Love Me Tender") which would be the NOW national anthem.

"Ain't That A Aham," (Formerly, "Ain't That A Shame") A new song telling the tale of the S & L bailout.

"The Great Offender," (Formerly, "The Great Pretender") Molly Yard's dedication to Rush Limbaugh.

"That'll Be The Day When I Fry," (Formerly, "That'll Be The Day When I Die") An anti capital punishment song that asks for more appeals before considering the death penalty.

"Born To Be Riled," (Formerly, "Born To Be Wild") The PC fight song.

"Sounds of Violence," (Formerly, "Sounds of Silence") A ballad justifying the festive mood of the looters during the LA riots.

45

Son of PC & Historical Revisionism

Historical revisionism has been the rage of multiculturalists who believe that women, minorities, and people with lifestyles different from the established norm have been underrepresented by historians. It is the intention of the proponents of political correctness to make all Americans aware of the contributions of these groups by rewriting textbooks and changing school curriculums. This involved altering public school history curriculums and begins with a thorough investigation into the text of our most famous historical documents. Below are samples of famous works that have been rewritten to make them more politically correct.

The Inscription on the Statue of Liberty
(from the poem "The New Colossus" by Emma Lazarus)

Give me your physically drained,
your monetarily subjugated,
Your huddled masses yearning
for political equality,
The misunderstood with alternative
lifestyles from your teeming shore.
Send these, the structurally denied
and emotionally disturbed to me,
I welcome with open arms, those with HIV
and all who are socially deplored.

The Gettysburg Address

Fourscore and seven years ago our progesterone dominant and testosterone driven ancestors brought forth on this continent a new nation, conceived with Eurocentric doctrines that denied everyone, except melanin negative males, the opportunity to grow as individuals. The traditionally oppressed must be given reparations if we are to be equal . . . that this secular nation, shall have a new direction; and the traditionally oppressed will force everyone else to conform to their way of thinking so we will have a government of the statistically burdened, by the culturally denied, and for the morally repressed regardless of what everyone else wants.

"Give Me Liberty or Give Me Death"
. . . Other women may cry peace, peace—but there is no peace. The war has actually begun. Our sisters are already in the field

fighting for equal rights, equal pay, and government paid abortions. Is life so dear, or peace so sweet, as to be purchased at the price of being a housewife? Forbid it, Almighty God! I know what course others may take; but as for me give me feminism, or give me death!

Abraham Lincoln's Second Inaugural Address

. . . With phallus toward none, with charity for all, with a staunch commitment toward secular humanism, let us finish the work we are in, to make the majority bend to the will of the minority, to create a government based on anarchy, to establish a socialist economic system, and to make all environmentalists, feminists, multiculturalists, animal rights activists, gay rights activists, homeless activists, comfortable in their desire to return America to its original state as a vast uninhabited region covered by ice and volcanic ash.

Push/Pull/Press

ORDER FORM

Phone orders by credit card: (800) 345-0096

P.O. Box 37175
Oak Park, MI 48237
FAX (313) 546-3010

QTY	TITLE	UNIT COST	TOTAL
	The Ultimate Dumb Blonde Joke Book	$6.95	
	The Politically Incorrect Joke Book	$6.95	
	Gifts I Almost Got You	$7.95	
	The Book of Cold War Nostalgia	$9.95	
		Subtotal	
		Shipping & Handling	
		MI residents add 4% sales tax	
		TOTAL	

Yes, please send me the books indicated above. Add $1.25 shipping and handling for the first book and .50 for each additional book. Add $2.00 to total for books shipped to Canada. Overseas postage will be billed. Allow up to 4 weeks for delivery. Send check or money order payable to Push/Pull/Press. No cash or C.O.D.'s please. Quantity discounts available upon request.

SEND BOOKS TO:

NAME: _____

ADDRESS: _____

CITY _____ STATE ___ ZIP ___